Dancing Round the Mango Tree

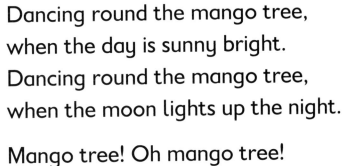

Dancing round the mango tree,
when the day is sunny bright.
Dancing round the mango tree,
when the moon lights up the night.

Mango tree! Oh mango tree!
Save your juicy fruit for me!

Dancing round the mango tree,
when the moon lights up the night.
Dancing round the mango tree,
now the day is sunny bright.

Mango tree! Oh mango tree!
Who came and stripped
the mango tree?

1

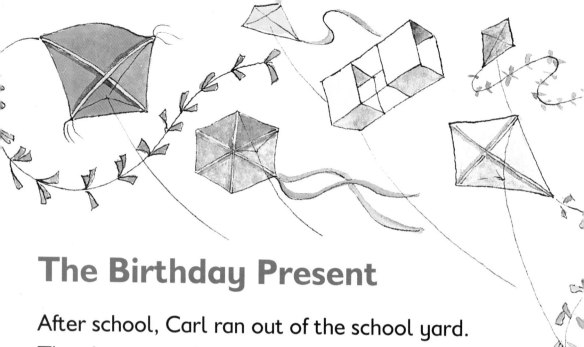

The Birthday Present

After school, Carl ran out of the school yard. Then he ran up the hill. He ran and ran until he got to the top.

   At the top of the hill, Carl looked up. There were lots of kites in the sky. There were big kites and small kites, new kites and old kites.

Carl didn't have a kite and he wanted one badly. He wanted a big one but his father said, "No. You are too small. Wait until you are older. Then you can have a big kite."

Carl said, "My birthday is next week. I will be older next week. Will you buy a big kite for me then?"

Carl's father said, "No, Carl. I can't buy a kite for you. Good kites cost a lot of money. I haven't got a lot of money. When I get some money, I will get you a fine, strong kite with a long tail."

So Carl asked, "Can I make a kite then?"
His father said, "No, Carl. You need a big, sharp knife to make a good, strong kite. You are too small to have a knife. Wait until you are older."

Carl looked at his father. Then he looked at his big brother, Paul. They looked very old.

He couldn't wait that long! Carl's father didn't ask him what he wanted for his birthday. His mother didn't ask him. Paul didn't ask him. Poor Carl. He only wanted one thing. A kite. But he was too small.

Carl ran inside to tell his mother about his friends Alan and Flo. They were in his class. Alan had a box kite. Flo had a big kite with a long tail that sang in the wind. Carl's mother hugged him and sent him to do his homework.

At last it was Carl's birthday.

"Happy birthday, Carl," said his mother and father.

"Happy birthday, Carl," said Paul. But they didn't give him a present.

Carl's father said, "You must come home quickly after school today, Carl. Please don't stop on the hill to look at the kites!"

WA Review punctuation: full stops, commas and exclamation marks. Point out the apostrophe, which stands in place of a missing vowel. Look at **-'s** as in **Carl's birthday** and **Carl's father**. Long ago, possession was shown by adding **es**, as in **Carles** birthday. The apostrophe that shows possession stands for that long lost **e**. Practise using possessive **-'s** with other nouns. **C** Why do you think Carl's parents waited till he came home to give him the kite?

At school, Carl was sad. He looked out of the window. The wind was blowing hard. It was a very good day for kites. He wanted to go and see them. Why did his father tell him not to stop on the hill to look at the kites?

After school, Carl ran home quickly. His mother and father and Paul were there.

"Come in, Carl. We have a present for you."

"What is it?" said Carl.

"Come in and look," said Paul.

On the table there was a very big butterfly. It was a butterfly made of paper and wood, a red and yellow butterfly with a long red tail.

"It's a kite!" shouted Carl. "It's a butterfly kite! But you said – "

"I didn't tell you because we wanted it to be a surprise," his father said. "I couldn't buy you a kite, but Mummy, Paul and I made one for you. It didn't cost a lot of money, and if it breaks, we can mend it."

"Thank you, thank you," said Carl. "Can I go up to the top of the hill and fly it?"

"Yes, Carl. Paul, Mummy and I worked hard on the kite, and we want to have fun with it too. So let's all go to the top of the hill and fly your kite!"

My Kite

I've got a fine red kite.
The tail is yellow bright.
Kite sails,
tail trails,
wind blows my fine red kite.

I've got a fine blue kite.
The tail is orange bright.
Kite sails,
tail trails,
wind blows my fine blue kite.

I've got a fine green kite.
The tail is purple bright.
Kite sails,
tail trails,
wind blows my fine green kite.

9

Flying

The next day Carl took his kite to school. He showed it to the class, and he showed it to Miss James.

Miss James said, "Let's talk about flying. Would you like to be able to fly?"

"Yes," May said. "I would like to go up in the sky. I would like to be a kite. A kite can see everything."

Indra said, "I would like to fly in a plane."

"So would I," said Carmen.

Carl said, "I would like to fly in a space ship."

"Good," said Miss James. "Now I want you to pretend you are flying in a space ship. Pretend you can see Earth. What does it look like?"

"It looks very funny," said Carmen. "The houses look like boxes."

"And the cars look like beetles," said Ben.

Then Miss James told them to write about their make-believe trip in a space ship. All the children wrote stories.

This is Indra's story.

WA What do **pretend**, **imagine** and **make believe** mean? Discuss **daydreams**. Who has daydreams? Why are they called daydreams? Was Carl daydreaming when he was thinking of the kites (p. 7)? **C** Why does May say that a kite can see everything? Why do **"houses look like boxes"** and **"cars look like beetles"**? **LP** Use drills and writing exercises to give practise in using irregular past tense forms, e.g., **said**, **told**, **took**, **wrote**. (See p. 48)

Out in Space

Vim, Jem and Tam are from outer space. They live on Mars. Mars is a planet that is very far away from Earth. One day, Vim went on a trip in his space ship. He went to look at Earth.

When he came back to Mars, Tam ran to him. She said, "We were looking for you. "Where did you go, Vim?"

"Out in space," said Vim. "I went to look at Earth."

"What did you see?" asked Jem.

"I saw people," said Vim.

Tam said, "You saw people? What are they like? What do they do?"

Vim said, "People are funny. They do funny things. They live in boxes."

"Oh, no!" said Tam. "Not in boxes!"

"Yes," said Vim, "and I saw things that looked like beetles."

LP Introduce the term **syllable**. Say the last three months of the year. Ask pupils to clap the beats in each month. How many are there? Pupils divide Oc/to/ber, No/vem/ber, De/cem/ber into syllables according to beats. Do the same with **funny, boxes, looking, yellow**. Pupils listen for the vowel sound in each word part. C Why does Vim think people live in boxes? Let pupils try to imagine what people live in on Mars.

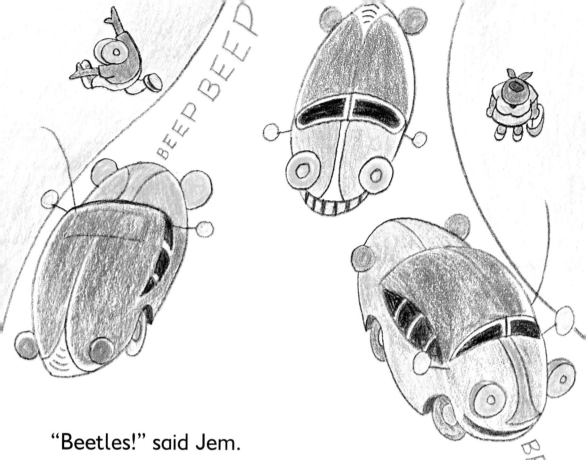

BEEP BEEP

BEEP BEEP

"Beetles!" said Jem.

"Yes," said Vim. "Some people ride in beetles."

"Oh, no!" said Jem. "Not in beetles."

"Yes," said Vim. "They ride about in funny beetles. The beetles talk. They say, 'beep, beep', and they have eyes. They have red eyes at the back, and they have bright yellow eyes at the front."

"You saw beetles that talk, beetles with bright yellow eyes!" said Tam.

Jem said, "I want to go out in space too. I want to see all the things you saw, Vim. Will you take me?"

"Take me too," said Tam. "I want to see people and boxes and beetles that talk."

"Let's go," said Vim.

So they climbed into Vim's space ship and away they went – Vim, Tam and Jem. Whoosh!

A Look at pictures of the solar system. Talk about the planets. What do pupils know about Mars?
PH Ask pupils to say the vowel sounds they hear in each of these words: **in**, **a**, **plan**, **fun**, **yell**, **beet**, **box**. Help pupils to find two-syllable words in the story (pp. 10–15) with each of the words **in**, **a**, **plan**, **fun**, **yell**, **beet** as one of the syllables. C What are the talking beetles? What are the red and yellow eyes?

15

"That was a good story," said Miss James. "Now I will tell you a story about a fish who wanted to fly. He wanted to be a bird."

Flin the Fish

Once there was a fish called Flin. Flin was a fish but he wanted to be a bird. He wanted to fly.

Flin swam to the top of the sea. He looked at the sky and he looked at the sea birds. Flin wanted to fly in the sky.

His friends told him, "If you go to the top of the sea, a sea bird will get you. That would be very bad."

"That would be very good," thought Flin. "If a bird gets me, it will take me up into the sky, and I will learn to fly."

Sea birds eat fish. But Flin didn't know this.

So Flin swam to the top of the sea. Every time he saw a sea bird he swam very fast and called, "Sea bird, sea bird, take me with you. Take me into the sky where I can learn to fly."

But Flin was blue and grey so the birds did not see him in the water. They did not eat him, and they did not help him to fly.

Flin looked at the birds every day. He looked at their wings. "My fins are like wings," he thought. "I can learn to fly."

"You are mad," his friends said. "You are a fish. Fish can't fly."

PH Add **Fl**, **th**, **sh**, **ch** to word part **-in**. Add **fl**, **sh**, **ch** to word parts **-ip** and **-op**. Give pupils practice in distinguishing between **sh** and **ch**. C Talk about Flin. Why did he think he could learn to fly? How do you think Flin felt when he found himself up in the air? Make a list of words and phrases. LP Revise exclamation marks. WA Put **saw**, **day**, **can**, **fly** on flash cards. Pupils join them with other words to make compound words.

But every day Flin swam to the top of the sea. He looked at the birds. He saw how they opened their wings. Flin thought, "I can learn to fly. My fins are like wings. If I swim very fast and open my fins, I will fly."

One day, he swam very, very fast, and he opened his fins.

Splash!

Flin came out of the sea.

Then Flin fell back into the sea.

Plop!

The next day he did it again. He swam very fast and he opened his fins.

Splash! Plop!

The next day he did it again. Flin zoomed out of the sea.

Splash! Whoosh!

"I'm a bird, I'm a bird," he shouted.

Flin fell back into the sea.

Plop!

Every day he flew out of the sea.

Splash! Whoosh!

But every day he fell back in.

Plop!

At last he thought, "I am not a bird. I can fly, but I am still a fish. I am a flying fish!"

Flin's friends came to see.

"Flin can fly!" they shouted. And they all wanted to learn. So Flin showed them how to fly.

Now all fish like Flin can fly. We call them flying fish. But Flin was the first.

The Airport

After school, Carl told his friends about his Uncle Ted.

"He is a pilot. He flies a plane," Carl said.

"How high does he fly?" Carmen asked.

"What does he see from the plane?" Indra asked.

"How does his plane stop? Has it got brakes like a car?" Ben asked.

"I'm not a pilot," Carl said. "I don't know. But we can ask Uncle Ted. He's taking me to the airport on Saturday. We can all go. He will tell us."

On Saturday, Uncle Ted came for Carl and his friends.

"Let's pretend," said Uncle Ted, "that this car is a plane and we are flying from Trinidad to Barbados. Fasten your seat belts. No smoking, please. Off we go!"

Uncle Ted started the car.

"How high are we?" asked Indra.

"Trinidad is close to Barbados, so we fly at 10,000 feet. There are lots of clouds today, so we can't see. On a clear day, I can see the rivers, roads and tree tops."

"Where did you go last week?" Indra asked.

"I went to Miami. That's in the United States."

"Did you go to England, too?" Carl asked.

"No, I didn't go to England. My plane is too small to fly to England."

WA Revise apostrophe as in **I'm**, **don't**, **he's** (p. 22) **let's**, **it's** (p. 23), **that's**, **didn't**, **we'll** (p. 24).
LP *Teacher*: My uncle flies. Does my uncle fly? *Pupils*: Does my uncle fly? *Teacher*: lands *Pupils*: Does my uncle land? *Teacher*: stops *Pupils*: Does my uncle stop? Use **talks**, **signals**, **goes**, **moves**, etc., to continue drill.

Soon Carl saw the airport. "We must land now," he said.

"Yes," said Ben. "Fasten your seat belts!"

Uncle Ted stopped the car. They all went into the airport. "We'll go and watch the planes," said Uncle Ted.

"There's a plane!" Carmen shouted.

"I can't see it," said Ben.

Carl said, "Yes, there it is. It is coming out of a cloud now."

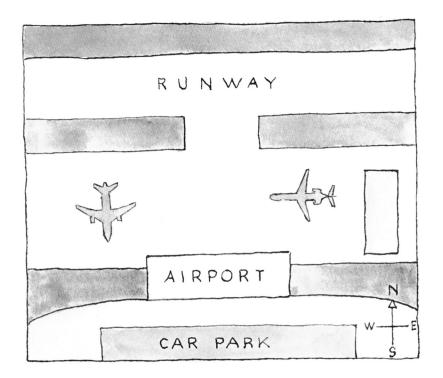

"You're right," said Uncle Ted. "Now watch it come down. Watch what the pilot does. He will slow the plane down. Then he will land on the runway between the rows of lights."

The children watched as the plane touched down.

"How does the pilot slow down the plane?" asked Indra. "A plane is so big."

C Look at the plan of the airport. Work out which direction is North. How does the runway go: from North to South or East to West? Where did they park the car? Where did the plane land? Where do you think they went to have a drink? WA Have pupils find and break down compound words **airport** (p. 24), **runway** (p. 25). A Draw a plan of your school and its surroundings.

25

"The pilot slows the engines, and he uses the flaps on the wings. The wind pushes against the flaps. They help to slow down the plane. When he lands, he uses the brakes on the wheels like the brakes on the wheels of a car."

The plane landed. It was a big jet.

What a noise it made!

After they watched some more planes for a while, they began to feel thirsty.

Uncle Ted took them inside the airport and got them a cold drink each.

"I want to go on a jet one day," said Ben.

"So do I," said Indra. "My uncle works in the United States. I will go and visit him."

When they went back to the car, Carl asked, "Is this car still a plane?"

"Yes," said Carmen. "So fasten your seat belts. This is a non-smoking flight."

"We're taking off!" they shouted.

PH Revise silent e rule as it applies to **plane**, **brake**, **made**. C At the end of the story, let pupils turn back to page 22 and answer Carl's friends' questions. LP *Teacher*: The plane slows down. *Pupils*: The plane slows down. *Teacher*: land *Pupils*: The plane lands. *Teacher*: stop *Pupils*: The plane stops. Use other cues like **turn**, **start**, **take off**, **fly**, **soar**, etc., to continue drill.

27

May Looks after the Shop

May was in her father's shop. Her father wasn't there. He was taking goods to people in the next road. Grandpa was asleep in the back room.

May was looking after the shop. She was putting things away.

She moved some boxes. She moved some bottles and tins. A man came in, but the work May was doing was noisy. She didn't hear him.

"Huh hum," the man said.

May jumped.

"All alone?" he said.

May turned and looked at the man. She didn't know him.

WA Revise use of apostrophe to show possession as in **father's**. **LP** *Teacher:* Work. May was working in the shop. *Pupils:* May was working in the shop. *Teacher:* sweep *Pupils:* May was sweeping in the shop. Use other cues like **dust, pack, add, help, clean, write, read, doze**, etc., to continue drill. **C** Why did May jump? Why do you think the man asked her if she was all alone?

29

"Yes, may I help you?" May said.

"I want a tin of milk."

May got the tin of milk.

"And I want some bread and some peas," the man said.

May got them. Then he wanted more.

"What a lot of things," May thought. She had never sold so many things. Her father would be pleased. May put them in a box.

The man turned. He went to the door.

"Hey!" May shouted. "You must pay for those goods."

The man looked at her. "No," he said. "I haven't got any money. Maybe I'll pay next week."

Then he saw the bottles.

"I want some beer," he said and he picked up a bottle of beer.

May moved fast. She pushed the boxes. She pushed the bottles of beer. Bang! Crash! Bang! Bottles and boxes and tins went everywhere.

C What did the man want? Why would May's father be pleased? **LP** *Teacher:* Yesterday and the day before, May shouted. Sometimes May shouts. *Pupils:* Sometimes May shouts. *Teacher:* Yesterday and the day before, May dozed. *Pupils:* Sometimes May dozes. *Teacher:* Yesterday and the day before, May cleaned. *Pupils:* Sometimes May cleans. Use **helped**, **worked**, **tried**, **packed** to continue drill.

31

"What are you doing?" the man shouted.

He turned to go but he tripped on a tin and fell over a box. He wanted to get up but he tripped on another box and fell over again.

May pushed more boxes and more tins.

Bang! Crash! Bang!

May's father ran into the shop.

"What a noise!" he said.

Then he saw the man. But the man got up quickly and ran away.

"Are you all right, May?" asked her father.

"Yes, I'm all right," May said.

"You were very brave," said her father, "but where is Grandpa?"

"Grandpa is in the back room. He was asleep. I think he is still asleep. You know Grandpa. Nothing wakes Grandpa!"

C Talk about whether May was really alone. How do you think May's father felt? (e.g., happy, angry, pleased, etc.) How do you think Grandpa felt when he woke up? LP *Teacher*: Nothing wakes Grandpa. *Pupils*: Nothing wakes Grandpa. *Teacher*: troubles *Pupils*: Nothing troubles Grandpa. Use **frightens**, **scares**, **tempts**, **provokes**, **surprises**, **amazes**, **annoys**, etc., to continue drill.

33

The next day, Carl and Ben went to the shop. May told them about the man, and about Grandpa.

May said, "Grandpa sleeps a lot, but he is a good friend. He is very old, but he can fix kites and plant corn. He knows the names of all the birds and he tells good stories."

Grandpa came out of the shop. He was going to the beach to mend fishing nets.

"Hello, children," he said. "I am going to the beach. Do you want to come with me?"

"Yes, please!" the children shouted.

"I will tell you a story on the way," Grandpa said. "I will tell you a story about Anancy."

Mr Anancy and the Corn

Long long ago, every animal had a farm. Mr Monkey had the best farm. He worked on his farm every day, and he had the best corn.

All the animals made paths to get to and from their farms, but Mr Monkey did not make a path. He was a monkey, and monkeys live in trees. So Mr Monkey jumped to and from his farm. He jumped from one tree top to the next. He went very fast.

One day, Mr Anancy found Mr Monkey's farm. When he saw the good corn, he said, "I wish I had some of that. I will ask the farmer to give me some."

"Good day, Mr Farmer," he called out. Nobody answered. Mr Anancy looked everywhere. The farm had no path. "There is no path to this farm," he thought. "It doesn't belong to anybody. I have found it, so it belongs to me."

C Who is Mr Anancy? Is this his usual title? Why didn't Mr Monkey make a path? Why did Mr Anancy think that the farm had no owner? **LP** Drill irregular past tense. Keep a steady, firm rhythm like a chant: *Teacher*: When I say, "**have**", you say "**had**". *Teacher*: have *Pupils*: had *Teacher*: have *Pupils*: had *Teacher*: When I say, "**go**", you say, "**went**". *Teacher*: go *Pupils*: went *Teacher*: go *Pupils*: went (Cont'd on p. 38.)

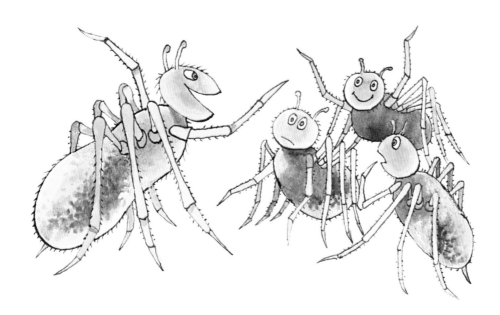

He went home and said to his children, "You must all come and help me."

"What do you want us to do?" they asked.

"Make a path," said Mr Anancy.

"A path? What for?" asked the children.

"I have found a farm. It has the best corn I have ever seen. There is no path to it, so it can't belong to anybody. If we make a path, it will be ours," Mr Anancy said.

Next day, they all went to work. Soon they had made the path. Then they cut some corn and took it home. They did this every day.

Mr Monkey saw that his corn was going. "I must find out who is taking it," he thought.

So Mr Monkey hid in a tree and watched. Soon he saw Mr Anancy and all his children.

"Stop!" Mr Monkey called out. "That is my corn. Why are you cutting it?"

"It's not yours," said Mr Anancy. "It's mine. I found it."

"But I planted it. This is my farm," said Mr Monkey.

"How can it be your farm? Where is the path?" asked Mr Anancy.

"I don't need a path. I jump through the tree tops," said Mr Monkey.

LP *Teacher:* When I say, "**see**", you say "**saw**". *Teacher:* see *Pupils:* saw *Teacher:* see *Pupils:* saw *Teacher:* When I say, "**is**", you say "**was**". *Teacher:* is *Pupils:* was *Teacher:* is *Pupils:* was. Use **find/found, say/said, come/came, take/took. hide/hid, fly/flew, make/made, think/thought, bring/brought, keep/kept,** etc., to continue drill. **C** How did Mr Monkey know Mr Anancy was taking his corn? Do you think Mr Owl's decision is right (p.39)?

"Tell that to Mr Owl. Let's see what he thinks,"
said Mr Anancy. "I made the path. So it is my corn."

When they asked him, Mr Owl said that farms
always have paths. Mr Anancy made the path so
the corn must be his. Mr Monkey felt very, very sad.
After all the hard work on his farm, he had to go
away. And now Mr Anancy had all his corn.

Mr Anancy was pleased. "Let's cut all the corn and
take it home quickly," he told his children.

They worked very fast. They cut all the corn and they started to take it home. But before they got home it began to rain.

"Put the corn under the trees. It will keep dry there. We will go into this hut," said Mr Anancy. "The rain will stop soon."

They waited for a long time. At last, the rain stopped. Mr Anancy said, "All right. Now we can go and get the corn."

They went back to the trees, but they found some big brown birds sitting with their wings over the corn.

C Before reading page 41, ask: "What do you think will happen next?" After reading page 41, ask: "Why did Mr Monkey laugh? What is the moral of this story?" LP *Teacher*: Today, Anancy finds a farm. Yesterday. *Pupils*: Yesterday, Anancy found a farm. *Teacher*: Today, Anancy sees corn. Yesterday. *Pupils*: Yesterday, Anancy saw corn. Continue drill with other sentences from the story.

"Thank you for keeping my corn dry for me," said Mr Anancy.

"It's not yours," said the birds. "It's ours. We found it, so it belongs to us."

Then the big brown birds picked up the corn and flew away with it. So Mr Anancy and his children had to go home with nothing.

"Hello, Mr Monkey! Hello!"

"Hello! Who is it?" asked Mr Monkey.

"It's your friends the brown birds. We brought back your corn."

"Thank you so much!" cried Mr Monkey.

And he laughed long and loud.

Fishing

When Grandpa and the children got to the beach,
Grandpa went to mend nets.

Carl had his fishing line. He wanted to fish.

"I am a great fisherman," he said. "Come and watch
me. I always catch lots of fish."

But Ben wanted to swim and May wanted to look for
shells.

"Oh no!" May suddenly shouted.

"What is it?" asked Ben.

"Look at these dead fish."

Ben looked at the dead fish. "Somebody caught some
fish, and left them on the beach," he said. Then he
picked them up.

"What are you doing?" May asked. "They smell bad."

"I have got a plan. Listen." And Ben told May his plan.

May went to the end of the jetty.

"Have you caught any fish?" she asked.

"No," said Carl. "I haven't caught any yet. But wait. I will catch some soon."

May sat next to him and they waited. Then something pulled Carl's line.

"There's a fish on the end of my line. Watch me. I'll pull it in. I think it's a big one," said Carl.

C Before reading this page, ask: What do you think Ben's plan is? Pupils read on to find out if they are right. LP Drill **think/thought, throw/threw, get/got, leave/left, catch/caught, tell/told, say/said**, using pattern in teacher's box on page 38. WA Find compound words **Grandpa, fisherman, somebody, something** on pages 42–43. Break them down. Find other words to go with each part, e.g., Grandma, workman, sometimes. C What is a jetty?

43

When Carl pulled up his line, there was a fine big fish on the end.

"Look at that!" he shouted. "It's a big one. I told you I would catch a big fish."

"It is big," May said. "But it looks dead. And it smells dead."

"Oh, no!" said Carl. "Well, I will catch another." Carl threw the dead fish back into the sea.

Soon Carl felt something pull the end of his line.

"I have got another fish. Watch! I'll pull it in." Carl pulled, and another big fish came out of the water.

"Look at that. It's another big one!" he shouted.

"It is big," said May. "But it looks dead. And it smells, too!"

"Oh, no! Not again," said Carl, and he threw the fish back. "I'll try again."

Once more Carl pulled up a big fish. But it was dead.

Then Carl saw Ben. Ben was under the jetty. He was laughing. May was laughing. Carl looked at them. Then he started to laugh, too.

He asked Ben, "Did you put dead fish on my line?"

"Yes," said Ben. "You told us you were a great fisherman. I thought you would be pleased to catch so many fish!"

C How did Carl know that Ben had tricked him? Was Carl angry? How do you know? LP *Teacher:* You put a fish on my line. Did you put a fish on my line? *Pupils:* Did you put a fish on my line? *Teacher:* You put a crab on my line. *Pupils:* Did you put a crab on my line? Use **lobster, snapper** and names of other fish to continue drill. A Have you ever played a trick on someone? How did the person feel about it?

Notes to Teachers

New Caribbean Readers 1, 2, 3A and *3B* are designed to appeal to pupils by offering them stories and rhymes that they will enjoy. Notes (on the inside front covers of all the books and at the end of 3A and 3B) are meant to help teachers, parents and pupils with suggestions for exercises in phonics (PH), numbering (N), comprehension (C), language practice (LP) and word attack skills (WA), as well as activities (A). This revision includes examples that refer to each book.

We know from recent research that:

- planning classes
- being positive and showing that you enjoy activities in the classroom
- being open to suggestions and willing to see pupils' points of view
- giving all pupils a chance to participate and giving each a chance to succeed
- creating an atmosphere that is secure
- using different teaching approaches

are characteristic of good teaching overall and of developing critical, creative and comprehension skills. So plan ahead. Be open. Be happy and receptive.

Extending students' responses. Illustrations are an integral part of the reading text. Have pupils talk about the pictures *before* reading to stimulate interest and introduce new vocabulary. Let them 'read' the pictures before the words and guess what will happen based on pictures, e.g., the pictures in *Mr Anancy and the Corn.* Ask them: "What happens to make Mr Monkey laugh and Anancy be so sad at the end of the story (p. 41)?" Pupils can develop their own ideas then read to find out if they are correct. They can compare/contrast things and people, identify colours, learn about perspective. Ask them: "Why does Carl look smaller than his father and brother on page 4, but bigger than they are on page 5?"

Pupils should feel free to express themselves. Create opportunities for them to exchange ideas. Ask them to comment on one another's suggestions. Postpone arriving at answers right away. This is modelling good thinking behaviour! Instead, ask them to think about tough questions as a homework assignment, or to do research by interviewing experts or consulting a book or the Internet. Urge them to consider all suggestions. Ask questions like "Do you think that would ever happen?" Give them choices so they know you respect their ideas.

Phonics. Even after they become confident readers, continue to observe how well students hear sounds. The ability to discriminate sounds in one language carries over to hearing sounds in other languages. Help pupils hear the sounds in their own language, e.g., Creole speakers sound **car** as *cyar*, **garage** as *gyarage*, etc. Many cannot hear initial **h**, and many sound initial **sn** as *s-n*, so *s-nake* for **snake**. Twisters in readers one and two can continue to be useful in sensitizing pupils to sound. Continue to ask pupils to read aloud, even when they are confident readers. Research has shown that reading aloud contributes to developing comprehension skills. Rules, like the rule for silent **e**, are very helpful. The Internet is a good source of handy rules – and their exceptions.

Punctuation has two functions: to make meaning clear, and to help the reader 'hum the tune' – that is, hear the right rhythms, pauses and stops. If the same words are punctuated differently, they mean differently, as this story shows. A panda goes to a café and orders a meal. When he's done, he takes out a gun, fires it into the air, and leaves. The manager rushes up and asks him why he's done this. The panda hands him a dictionary and says, "It's because I'm a panda. Here. Look it up." When the manager does, he sees that the dictionary says a panda is 'an animal that eats shoots and leaves'! Punctuation makes the difference between, e.g., "Come Pam," and "Come, Pam!" Use raps, skits and jingles to teach the use of commas, full stops, apostrophes, exclamation marks, etc. Let pupils punctuate humorous examples of ambiguous sentences and take turns saying sentences with and without appropriate punctuation.

Remind pupils often of what capital letters are used for. This is a good place to explain how we have used capitals in the titles of each story in these readers. We've used capital letters for important words in the title, like names (e.g., *Flin the Fish* on page 16). We've also capitalized the first and last words in every title, no matter how short or insignificant they are.

This is also a good place to explain that we have used the modern style of punctuation for abbreviations like Mr (Mister), Dr (Doctor), St (Saint), etc. The new rule is to omit the full stop if the abbreviation is represented by the first and last letters of the full word, e.g., Mr for <u>Mister</u>. If an abbreviation is not made up of the first and last letters of the full word, then a full stop is needed, e.g., Ave. for <u>Ave</u>nue and St. for <u>St</u>reet.

Creative activities help pupils to embed what they understand. Many examples are given here. They can make up and illustrate poems and stories; act out stories, e.g., *Mr Anancy and the Corn*; make and mount displays. Remember, imagining is part of understanding!

Poetry. Pupils should relate what happens in poems (and stories) to events in their lives. For example, ask pupils whether they have ever had an experience like the one described in *Dancing Round the Mango Tree* (p.1). Beat or clap out the rhythm in poems, and sound out the rhymes. Make up a tune and dance to the poem; use suitable poems as models; write poems in response to another poem, or to a story, as in the activity in the teachers' box on page 21. (Poems don't have to rhyme.) Encourage pupils to think of what they see, hear, feel, when they read a poem and to describe these responses when they write one. Build on the poems in this book by starting a poetry bank. Ask pupils to bring their favourite poems to school and share yours with them. Many lullabies, hymns, folk songs etc., are great poems. Twisters are good models for pupils to write their own sound poems.

Language practice. Put drills into meaningful contexts by (1) choosing the structure from a story being read in class, (2) making the drill into a skit, a chant (e.g., the exercise in the teachers' boxes on pages 36 and 38) or a song. Divide the class into two. One side asks questions, the other responds. Switch sides. Make it fun by having them say the cues and responses like different characters, e.g., Grandpa, Anancy, etc. Make sure you prepare many cues! Some more examples of drills are included on the back cover.